THE NFL
DRAFT

ELLIOTT
1

D1157914

DiscoverRoo
An Imprint of Pop!
popbooksonline.com

Robert Cooper

abdobooks.com

Published by Pop!, a division of ABDO, PO Box 398166, Minneapolis, Minnesota 55439. Copyright © 2020 by POP, LLC. International copyrights reserved in all countries. No part of this book may be reproduced in any form without written permission from the publisher. Pop!™ is a trademark and logo of POP, LLC.

Printed in the United States of America, North Mankato, Minnesota.

052019
092019

THIS BOOK CONTAINS RECYCLED MATERIALS

Cover Photo: Perry Knotts/AP Images
Interior Photos: Perry Knotts/AP Images, 1, 17 (bottom), 31; Ben Liebenberg/AP Images, 5, 22; Aaron M. Sprecher/AP Images, 6–7, 17 (top); Mark Humphrey/AP Images, 8; Albert Pena/Cal Sport Media/AP Images, 9, 30; David Stluka/AP Images, 11; Shutterstock Images, 12–13; Michael Conroy/AP Images, 14, 15; David J. Phillip/AP Images, 16 (top); Butch Dill/AP Images, 16 (bottom); AP Images, 19; NFL Photos/AP Images, 20; Paul Spinelli/AP Images, 21; Albert Pena/Cal Sport Media/AP Images, 23; Robin Alam/Icon Sportswire/AP Images,
25; Cory Dellenbach/Shawano Leader/AP Images, 26; Allen Kee/AP Images, 27; Margaret Bowles/AP Images, 28–29

Editor: Nick Rebman
Series Designer: Jake Nordby

Library of Congress Control Number: 2018964850
Publisher's Cataloging-in-Publication Data

Names: Cooper, Robert, author.
Title: The NFL draft / by Robert Cooper.
Description: Minneapolis, Minnesota : Pop!, 2020 | Series: Football in America | Includes online resources and index.
Identifiers: ISBN 9781532163784 (lib. bdg.) | ISBN 9781644940518 (pbk.) | ISBN 9781532165221 (ebook)
Subjects: LCSH: Football--Juvenile literature. | American football--Juvenile literature. | National Football League--Juvenile literature. | Football draft--Juvenile literature.
Classification: DDC 796.33264--dc23

WELCOME TO DiscoverRoo!

Pop open this book and you'll find QR codes loaded with information, so you can learn even more!

Scan this code* and others like it while you read, or visit the website below to make this book pop!

popbooksonline.com/nfl-draft

*Scanning QR codes requires a web-enabled smart device with a QR code reader app and a camera.

TABLE OF CONTENTS

CHAPTER 1
DRAFT DAY

Carson Wentz smiled as he held up his

new Philadelphia Eagles jersey. Cameras

flashed, and the crowd cheered. At

North Dakota State, Wentz had been

a college star. And on this day, he

WATCH A
VIDEO HERE!

Carson Wentz was the second player selected in the 2016 NFL Draft.

became a player in the National Football

League (NFL).

The NFL has 32 teams. Each year,

these teams come together for the

DID YOU KNOW? Each year, more than 200 players are selected at the **NFL Draft.**

During the draft, each team has a desk where team leaders make decisions.

NFL Draft. In this event, teams choose new members. They pick the very best college players.

The Los Angeles Rams chose quarterback Jared Goff with the first pick in the 2016 draft.

The draft has seven rounds. Every team gets one pick in each round. The order is based on each team's **record** from the year before. The team with the

worst record picks first. The Super Bowl winner picks last. That way, the worst teams get the best players.

New York Giants fans cheer after their team selects a player in the 2018 draft.

CHAPTER 2
GETTING READY

NFL teams send **scouts** to look for the best players. Scouts often travel to colleges to watch football games. More than 70,000 athletes play college football each year. But fewer than 2,000 of them will reach the pro level.

LEARN MORE HERE!

Scouts attend many college football games to see how players perform.

If a player wants to be selected by an NFL team, the months before the draft are important. Players go to **camps** and workouts. They show their

Some players push heavy sleds to build strength.

skills to NFL teams. They also work

with **trainers** to improve skills such as

catching and running.

The biggest event before the draft is the combine. College players and teams come together. The players are tested on many skills. They run, jump, and lift weights. Teams also meet with players to get to know them better.

Defensive back Sheldrick Redwine runs a drill at the 2019 combine.

Defensive back Hamp Cheevers tries to impress the scouts at the 2019 combine.

TIMELINE

EARLY JANUARY

The college football season ends.

MID-JANUARY

Players must decide if they are going to enter the draft.

LATE JANUARY

Top college players take part in the Senior Bowl, where they can show off in front of NFL scouts.

LATE FEBRUARY TO EARLY MARCH

The combine takes place.

ALL THROUGH MARCH

Players hold pro days at their colleges so that NFL teams can watch them work out.

LATE APRIL

The NFL Draft takes place.

CHAPTER 3
BECOMING A MAJOR EVENT

The first NFL Draft took place in 1936. Back then, most teams didn't know much about the players they chose. And the draft was not a popular event. People read about the results in the newspaper a few days later.

COMPLETE AN ACTIVITY HERE!

Philadelphia Eagles running back Jay Berwanger was the first player chosen in the 1936 draft.

Running back George Rogers smiles after being drafted by the New Orleans Saints in 1981.

TV reporter Chris Berman covers the 1987 draft for ESPN.

In the 1980s, the draft was shown on TV for the first time. More people began paying attention to it. Fans and reporters enjoyed guessing which players would end up on which teams.

The draft is now a big event that goes for three days. The first round lasts one night. It takes about four hours to complete. Thousands of fans go to see it in person.

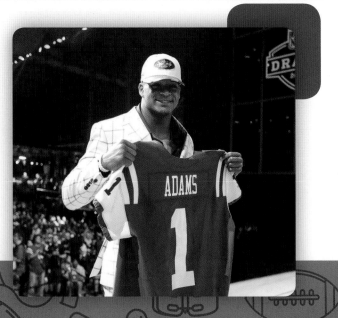

Jamal Adams poses with his new Jets jersey after being drafted in 2017.

UP NEXT: 54 CIN   55 CAR   56 TB   57 OAK   58

Fans pack AT&T Stadium to watch the 2018 draft.

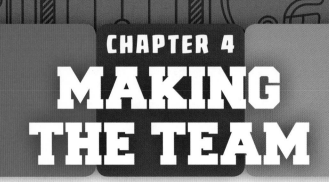

CHAPTER 4
MAKING THE TEAM

When the draft is over, players begin their NFL careers. They travel to their new team's city. They meet their coaches and talk with the **media**. Players might also get a jersey from the team.

LEARN MORE HERE!

Quarterback Mitchell Trubisky talks to reporters after being drafted by the Chicago Bears in 2017.

Members of the Green Bay Packers take part in a drill during training camp.

Then it's time to get to work. Teams hold **camps** for their **rookies**. These practices give the new guys a chance to learn about the team's plays.

St. Louis Rams legend Kurt Warner was undrafted but went on to win the Super Bowl.

After the camp, players go home to prepare for the season. They must be in good shape when full-team practices begin later in the summer. When

The first game of the season is exciting for all players, especially rookies.

practice starts, the rookies are one step

closer to playing in their first NFL game.

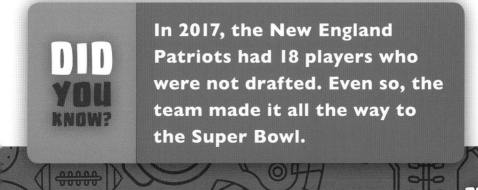

DID YOU KNOW?

In 2017, the New England Patriots had 18 players who were not drafted. Even so, the team made it all the way to the Super Bowl.

MAKING CONNECTIONS

TEXT-TO-SELF

Do you plan to watch the next NFL Draft? Why or why not?

TEXT-TO-TEXT

Have you read other books about the NFL? What did those books say about the NFL Draft?

TEXT-TO-WORLD

Thousands of football fans watch the draft each year on TV. Why do you think it's more popular today than it was in the 1930s?

GLOSSARY

camp – a series of practices to help players stay in shape and improve their skills.

media – groups that report the news.

record – the number of wins and losses a team has during a season.

rookie – a player in his or her first year in a sports league.

scout – a person who looks for talented young players.

trainer – a person who helps athletes stay in the best physical shape.

INDEX

ONLINE RESOURCES
popbooksonline.com

Scan this code* and others
like it while you read, or visit
the website below to make
this book pop!

popbooksonline.com/nfl-draft

*Scanning QR codes requires a web-enabled smart device with a QR code reader app and a camera.